Little Wolf and Smellybreff

Badness For Beginners

For Teddy and Ella –
who never get spoilt rotten, hem hem –
with love from You-Know-Who.

First published in paperback in Great Britain by HarperCollins Children's Books in 2005

1 3 5 7 9 10 8 6 4 2

ISBN: 0-00-714361-3

Text copyright Ian Whybrow © 2005
Illustrations copyright Tony Ross © 2005

HarperCollins Children's Books is a division of HarperCollins Publishers Ltd.

Visit our website address at: www.harpercollinschildrensbooks.co.uk

Printed and bound in Singapore

Little Wolf and Smellybreff

Badness for Beginners

Ian Whybrow + Tony Ross

HarperCollins *Children's Books*

In a nice smelly lair, far away, lived the Wolf family.
There was Mum Wolf, Dad Wolf, Little Wolf and
Baby Wolf. (He was the smelliest, so they
called him Smellybreff).

Mum and Dad were very proud of being big and bad.
They wanted Little and Smellybreff to grow
up big and bad like them.

Mum and Dad taught the cubs Naughty Nursery Rhymes.
Their favourite was "Never Say Thank You".

Never say thank you
Play with your food
Make all your noises
Naughty and rude

Talk with your mouth full
Answer back quick
Never stop eating
till you feel sick

Smellybreff was a quick learner; he was full of Badness.

But sometimes Little was good by mistake.

One day, Mum and Dad decided to teach Little and Smells
some more Badness lessons. Off they went to town.
"Remember," said Dad. "You must BOTH
be on your worst behaviour."

The Wolf family came to a bridge that was being mended.
Dad said, "Watch me!"

He went, "GURRR!" and scared the menders away.

He kicked over their Danger sign.

He kicked over their warning lights and he ate their sandwiches.

Mum said, "Well done, Dad! That was very nasty and horrible! What a fine example to the cubs!"

Smellybreff wanted to be nasty and horrible like his Dad.
Little said, "No, Smells, you are only a baby. Watch me!"

He made a mud pie in the road.
(It wasn't a very bad thing to do, but Little was trying his hardest.)

Smellybreff
went screamy-scream.

Then he jumped on
the menders' drill and went...

BRRR

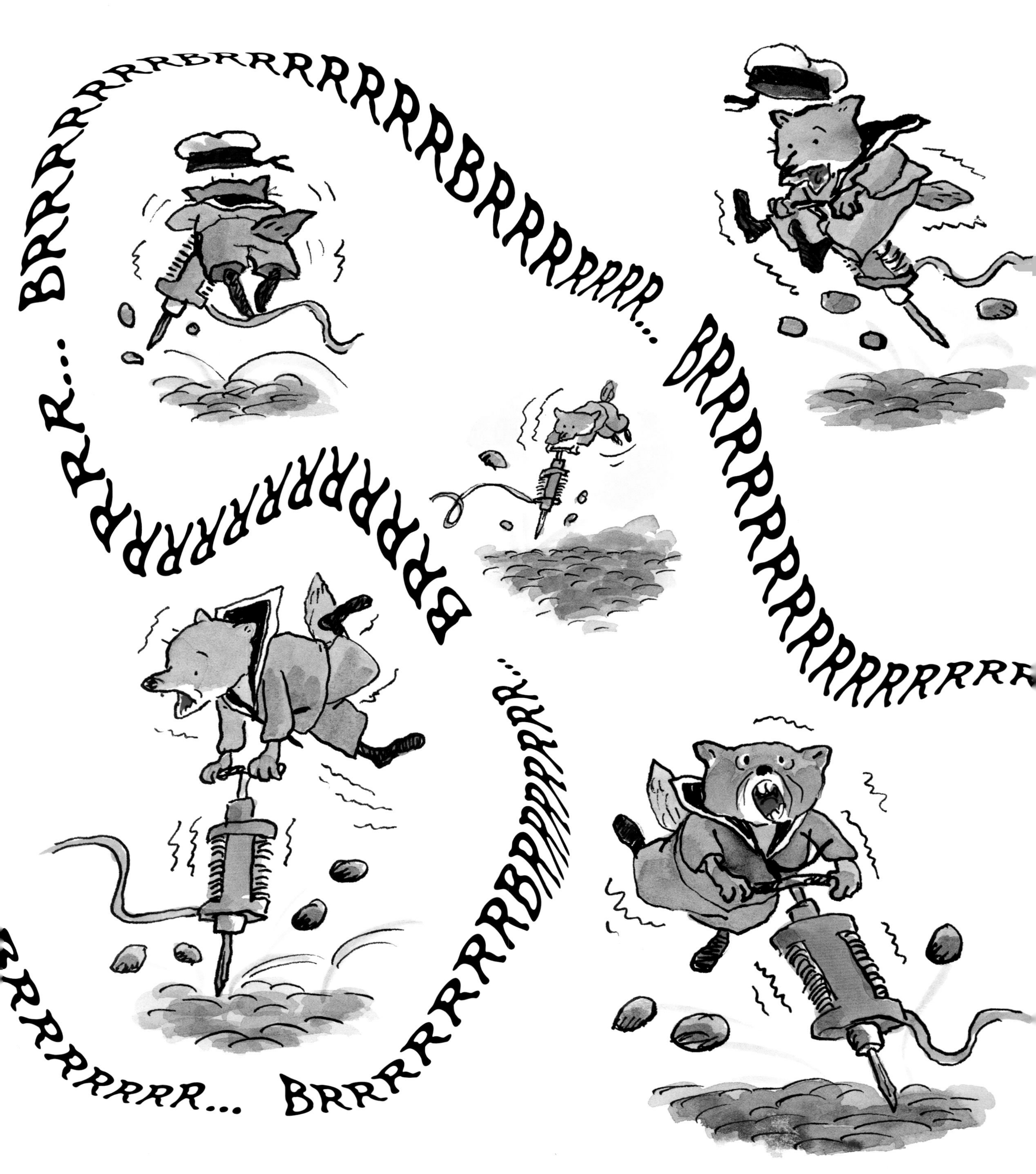

Soon there was a big hole.
"Well done, Smells!" said Mum. "What a clever cub!"

"For your next Badness lesson," said Dad,
"We'll go to the café."
"Ooh, THANKS, Dad!" said Little.
"Gurrr!" said Dad. "Stop being so polite, Little!
Why can't you learn to misbehave?"

At the café, Little tried really
hard to be bad. Out went his
tongue, wiggle, wiggle.
"Poor little cubby, you
must be thirsty," said
the waitress.

She patted him on the
head and gave him a nice
cold milk shake.

Smells went screamy-scream,
until he got a milk shake too.
He gulped it down in one go...

Then he went...

BBBBBBBBBBBURPPPP!

"Well done, our darling baby pet!"
said Mum and Dad. "That was very bad."

"I will try being bad one more time!" said Little.
He jumped up and went, "Gurrr!"
"Oh, what a lovely smile, little cubby!" said the waitress.
She patted him on the head and gave him a doggy choc.

Smellybreff was getting hungry.
He ate four banana splits and
a knickerbocker glory!

Then he was sick on the floor.
"What a clever cub!"
said Mum.

Along came the waitress, with soapy
water in a bucket, to clean up the mess.
Out went Smellybreff's naughty tail.

WHOOPS!

went the waitress.

"**OUT!**" shouted the waitress. "Go away, you horrible animals and never-never-never come back!"
She chased them all the way to the bridge.

By then it was getting dark.
There was no Danger sign.
And there were no
warning lights.

"AAH!" went Mum as she tripped on Little Wolf's mud pie.

"WHOAAA!" went Dad as he fell through the hole that Smellybreff had made.

Dad crawled back on to the bridge.
Little said, "Arrroooo! Smellybreff made a nice
big hole in the road. And my mud pie made Mum
slip over and knock you down it, Dad!"

Back at the lair, Little said, "What a lot we learned about Badness today, Mum and Dad! Will you teach me and Smells loads more tomorrow!"

All Mum and Dad could say was

"GURRR!"

So, Little sang this naughty lullaby
to make Mum and Dad feel better:

Hushaby, wolf cub,
Please do not snore –
Or I will shut your
Tail in the door.
Mummy and Daddy
Both need a rest.
Wait till tomorrow –
Then be a pest!

Plink!

Author:

Fiona Macdonald studied history at
Cambridge University, England, and at the
University of East Anglia. She has taught in
schools, adult education and universities, and
is the author of numerous books for children
on historical topics.

Artist:

David Antram was born in Brighton, England,
in 1958. He studied at Eastbourne College of Art
and then worked in advertising for fifteen years
before becoming a full-time artist. He has
illustrated many children's non-fiction books.

Series creator:

David Salariya was born in Dundee, Scotland.
He has illustrated a wide range of books and has
created and designed many new series for
publishers in the UK and overseas. David
established The Salariya Book Company in 1989.
He lives in Brighton, England, with his wife,
illustrator Shirley Willis, and their son Jonathan.

Editor: **Stephen Haynes**

Editorial Assistant: **Mark Williams**

PAPER FROM
SUSTAINABLE
FORESTS

Published in Great Britain in MMX by
Book House, an imprint of
The Salariya Book Company Ltd
25 Marlborough Place, Brighton BN1 1UB
www.salariya.com
www.book-house.co.uk

HB ISBN-13: 978-1-906714-25-3
PB ISBN-13: 978-1-906714-26-0

S A L A R I Y A

1 3 5 7 9 8 6 4 2

A CIP catalogue record for this book is available
from the British Library.

Printed and bound in China.

Visit our website at **www.book-house.co.uk**
or go to **www.salariya.com** for **free** electronic versions of:
You Wouldn't Want to be an Egyptian Mummy!
You Wouldn't Want to be a Roman Gladiator!
You Wouldn't Want to be a Polar Explorer!
You Wouldn't Want to sail on a 19th-Century
Whaling Ship!

Avoid working on a Medieval Cathedral!

Written by
Fiona Macdonald

Illustrated by
David Antram

Created and designed by
David Salariya

The Danger Zone™

BOOK HOUSE

Contents

Introduction   5

A grand tradition   6

Long-term project   8

Are you a good team player?   10

Learning on the job   12

Have mallet, will travel   14

Practice makes perfect   16

Grand designs   18

Health and safety   20

Dare you argue with an abbot?   22

Only the best will do   24

Pestered by pilgrims   26

Building for the future   28

Glossary   30

Index   32

Introduction

Hello there! Welcome to Canterbury! It's an ancient city and home to England's most important cathedral. Travellers come from far and wide to see it.

Come and meet my grandson. Over here, lad, and say hello! He'll be twelve next birthday – born around 1370, if my memory's right. Soon it will be time for him to start work.

Have you chosen a career yet, laddie? Eh? Eh? You want to be a builder, like your father and like me, your old grandpapa? Well, it's a good job, the pay's not bad, and you could work with us, of course. But what's that you say? You want to be an expert, top-class, the best...

You want to be a cathedral builder?

A grand tradition

So you think everyday buildings are boring and dull – just plain walls and windows and doorways? Well, cathedrals are certainly much more exciting. They're designed in the latest, daring styles and use only the very best materials. And, of course, they're always being made bigger and more beautiful.

What are cathedrals for? Why, surely you know that! They're huge, rich churches, where Christians worship God and think about heaven. And they're also bases for busy, bossy bishops.

Cathedral building would be a thrilling job, but, believe me, it's not easy. You'd need years of training and hard work, as well as natural talent. Do you think you're ready for that challenge?

Durham, England
c.1093–1133

Canterbury

YOU LIVE HERE

Notre Dame, Paris, France c.1163–1240

Santiago de Compostela, Spain c.1075–1128

What is a cathedral?

HOLY THRONE. The word *cathedral* comes from *cathedra*, the Latin (and Greek) name for a bishop's throne.

HOUSE OF GOD. To Christians, cathedrals are full of God's Holy Spirit. They are beautiful, holy places to say prayers.

STATUS SYMBOL. Grand and glorious, cathedrals are prestige buildings. Every big city wants one; so do its citizens.

Cathedrals are the finest buildings in Europe, magnificently decorated with carvings, coloured glass, glittering jewels and sculptures. They don't all look the same: each is a unique, inspiring work of art. Here are just a few of the most famous.

Speyer, Germany
c.1030–1100

St Mark's, Venice, Italy
c.832–1250

Pisa, Italy
c.1030–1250

Handy hint

Build with the best! Most people live in fragile timber buildings that don't last long. But cathedrals are made of stone, and designed to last for ever!

BAND OF BROTHERS. Some cathedrals also have a monastery attached. Brotherhoods of monks live there, devoting their lives to God. They take part in cathedral prayers and sing in cathedral choirs.

ROYAL CONNECTIONS. Kings are crowned in cathedrals. They hope that God will help them rule, and protect them.

The story so far

BY THE 14th CENTURY, Canterbury Cathedral already has a history stretching back hundreds of years.

1. c. AD 597–602. First cathedral built by St Augustine using remains of old Roman church; later rebuilt twice. Burned down by Vikings in 1011 (they later murder the archbishop, St Alphege); rebuilt again by 1038.

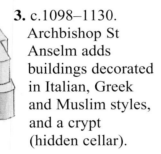

2. c.1067–1077. Cathedral again destroyed by fire, and replaced by new-style building planned by Archbishop Lanfranc, from France.

3. c.1098–1130. Archbishop St Anselm adds buildings decorated in Italian, Greek and Muslim styles, and a crypt (hidden cellar).

Long-term project

Tell me, my lad, how big is our house? Yes, four rooms, an attic and a workshop. And we are well off; most people nowadays live in cottages with one or two rooms.

Now, compare those homes with Canterbury Cathedral over there, towering above them. It's gigantic! It has pillars and arches, porches and niches, vast windows, steep roofs – and much more! Just think how complicated it was to design each part – and how long it took to construct them all! Cathedral-building takes centuries. It's a very slow process, aiming for perfection!

4. c.1174–1180. Another fire, and more rebuilding. A second crypt is added, plus new chapels. One houses the shrine of St Thomas Becket (see page 22).

5. c.1377–1410. The nave (main hall) of the cathedral is to be replaced by a splendid new one, with wonderful arches and carvings and a vaulted roof (see page 19).

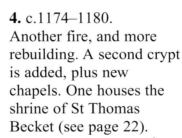

Angel Steeple

Canterbury Cathedral is 160 metres long, 47 metres wide and 72 metres high to the tip of its Angel Steeple.

Handy hint

Make friends with the rich and famous! New buildings at Canterbury are being paid for by a wealthy well-wisher.

You won't see another one like it anywhere!

9

Are you a good team player?

Meet the team

DEVISER. Designs each new section of the cathedral building, and marks out full-size patterns on the floor for masons and carvers to follow.

I t takes hundreds of people, all with different skills, to create a cathedral. If you want to share in their grand project, you must learn to work with them all. Learn to give and take, be cheerful and polite. If you help others, they'll help you! But if you're rude or lazy, expect big trouble.

All cathedral builders are respected for the quality of their work. Their skills and knowledge are essential. Which building craft will you choose to learn? None of them is easy!

Ow!

WOODCARVER (below). Uses razor-sharp tools to decorate doors, seats, screens and pulpits with wonderful shapes and patterns.

Aaargh!

QUARRYMAN. Hacks huge lumps of rock from cliffs and crags, and hammers them into rough slabs ready for the masons.

WOODWORKERS. Sawyers saw tall tree-trunks into neat planks. Joiners make doors and window frames. Skilled carpenters build rafters and scaffolding.

Wheeze!

MASON (left). Some masons shape rough-cut stone into precise building blocks. Others decorate them with carvings. It's a dusty job!

10

How's that window going to fit into this frame?

If you get shirty with me I'll report you to the guild!

Handy hint

Join a craftsman's guild. There's one for each trade. In most cities, you can't get a skilled job without being a guild member.

Do you have the muscle power?

In the 14th century there are no power tools or engines. You must construct buildings by hand, using simple technology and an enormous amount of muscle power. Cathedral builders must be tough, hard-working and strong!

He might have what it takes...

ROOFER (left). Covers wooden roofs with sheets of lead, or tiles made from slate or stone, to keep out rain and snow.

GLAZIER (below). Creates glorious windows using jagged pieces of coloured glass held in place by lead borders.

BELL-MAKER. Pours molten bronze into moulds dug in the ground to make clanging bells that call worshippers to the cathedral.

Learning on the job

Now you're for it!

Y ou say you'd like to be a stonemason. That's a good idea, but, whatever skill you decide to learn, you'll need a master to teach you. For seven years, you must promise to study, work hard and obey him. You'll live in his house as an apprentice – part pupil, part servant. You'll run errands, watch your master work, and ask lots of questions. The master will teach you all you need to know, from roughly shaping stone to carving delicate details. When the apprenticeship ends, you'll be older and wiser, and you'll graduate as a journeyman. Then you can work for anyone you choose, and you'll be paid by the day.

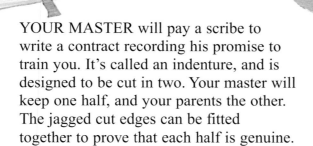

YOUR MASTER will pay a scribe to write a contract recording his promise to train you. It's called an indenture, and is designed to be cut in two. Your master will keep one half, and your parents the other. The jagged cut edges can be fitted together to prove that each half is genuine.

Crack!

13

Have mallet, will travel

Now, imagine that you're a journeyman. You're almost 20 years old, with no home, no food, no money – and no master to guide you. You're trained, but have no experience.

SAY GOODBYE to your master. He's taught you all he can. Now you must fend for yourself. Get ready – and get going!

Take an old man's advice, my lad! You need hard work, boring work – and plenty of it. Find whatever building job you can, and learn day by day. Build up your knowledge, your savings and your strength. Then, perhaps, a team of cathedral builders might be willing to employ you.

Summer sun

Spring showers

Kyrie eleison!
(Lord, have mercy on us!)

Way-hey!

ROUSED BY NOISY REVELLERS at a busy roadside inn? Pull the blankets over your ears and try to ignore them!

Life on the road

LOOKING FOR LODGINGS at the local monastery? Remember, monks get up at midnight to chant their first prayers of the morning!

Autumn gales

AS A JOURNEYMAN, you may work on a project for days, weeks or years, until your task is completed. But then you'll need to find new work again, and quickly! Be prepared to walk miles between building sites – and to face tough travel conditions.

Handy hint

Make friends with senior stonemasons. They might shelter you in their _mansione_ (workroom and dormitory) on the building site.

WOOOOooo

CROUCHED IN A CHURCH PORCH? Then you'll need strong nerves. Bats, owls and other creatures of the night have a habit of lurking there.

Winter snows

Wakey wakey!

Snort!

SEEKING SHELTER with peasants? Poor families bring their livestock indoors – and some creatures can get _far_ too close for comfort!

BEDDED DOWN IN A BARN? Then beware of the bull and other big animals sheltering there. They may not welcome sharing their space with sleepy strangers!

Practice makes perfect

Think ahead ten more years. You've survived as a travelling journeyman. It's been a tough life, but you've learned a lot from your workmates and from the sights you've seen on your travels. Your next step will be to apply for a job on site at Canterbury Cathedral.

But what's this splendid statue you've been working on secretly? Aha! It's your test-piece! I hope the craftsmen's jury likes it, because, if they do, you'll qualify as a proper master mason. You'll win prestige, more money, and respect from your friends and neighbours. Even more important, you'll get the chance to work on all kinds of cathedral stonework.

Will you pass the test?

A JURY of expert stonemasons will examine your test sculpture. Will they find fault and reject it – or praise it as your masterpiece?

Of course, it's a bit modern for my taste.

Nice work, though.

GARGOYLES. These funny, scary faces (1) hide pipes that carry rainwater away from the walls and roofs.

BUTTRESSES (2) prevent high walls from leaning outwards.

STATUES of favourite saints (3) remind worshippers of heaven.

ARCHES (4) hold up roofs and floors. Until around 1150, arches were made wide and rounded. Now, in the 1380s, they are narrow and pointed.

PILLARS support the arches. Most have decorated capitals at the top (5). Their shafts (uprights) may be carved to look like narrow columns side by side (6). Sometimes they are multi-coloured.

CARVED FRIEZES decorate the walls, inside and out (7).

STONE SLABS OR TILES cover the floor (8). There might also be a maze – a symbol of the soul's search for God.

Read the 'Poor Man's Bible'. That's the name for glowing stained-glass windows that tell Bible stories in pictures.

Do you think you could do that?

Just let me try!

Shining example

Henry Yevele, the greatest master mason in England, arrived in Canterbury not long ago (c.1377) to work on the cathedral's new nave and monks' cloisters (courtyard). Yevele is already famous for building royal palaces and castles. So aim high – watch and copy him. It's the chance of a lifetime!

17

Grand designs

What next? Why not apply to help a famous master mason design a new chapel? If you get that job, you really will have reached the top of your profession!*

You'll have big responsibilities, too. Design mistakes can lead to terrible disasters. Have you heard of Ely Cathedral? In 1322, a badly designed stone tower crashed through its roof to the floor!

With luck, your new master will show you how to create exciting new designs. You'll study old buildings, make lots of measurements, and draw sketches. Some masons base their plans on mysterious mathematical calculations. They say that these contain holy secrets!

* It's the 14th century, and architects have not yet been invented.

Dual purpose

Flying buttress

Nave wall

MANY CATHEDRAL FEATURES are designed with a double purpose: to be useful *and* look good. Graceful 'flying buttresses' support walls without blocking the light from the windows.

18   KEEP A SKETCHBOOK, as French artist Villard de Honnecourt did in the 13th century.

BE BOLD! EXPERIMENT! Make trial drawings of your own building plans on a drawing-floor covered with wet plaster.

SLIM PINNACLES add weight to stonework to make it more stable.

Pinnacle

Top of buttress

RIB-VAULTING spreads the weight of the ceiling and carries it down to the ground.

Vault

Ribs

Pillars

Handy hint

Make good foundations, or your building will never stand straight. Look at the famous Leaning Tower at Pisa Cathedral in Italy. It's built on sand!

We'll have to get the builders in again.

Ely Cathedral, 1322: The central tower gives way, after standing for 200 years. It's lucky that no-one's killed.

19

Health and safety

If you become a master mason yourself, it'll be your job to plan and manage all the different stages of the building. You must organise your masons: some will 'set out' (make templates for others to copy); others, less skilled, will saw and 'bank' (rough-cut) blocks into shape, ready for expert carver-masons to create the finished stonework. You must also give orders to the other craftsmen on site – and keep tight control of the budget!

At times, you'll get tired and stressed, but don't put your own life in danger. Remember what happened to master mason William of Sens, right here in Canterbury. He climbed 15 metres up to examine some stonework – and fell off the scaffolding!

DUST stings eyes, scratches noses, tickles throats and chokes lungs.

CARRYING HEAVY LOADS wears out joints, most painfully.

BACKACHE comes from a life spent crouched over carvings.

Creak

POISONOUS LEAD makes roofers and glaziers very, very ill.

GLASS FURNACES glow red-hot. They burn and blister. Ow!

Retired hurt

At first, William of Sens tried to keep on working from his sickbed. But he was too ill, and soon left Canterbury for France, his homeland. He died there in 1180, a year after his accident. His designs were completed by a new master mason, William the Englishman, in 1184.

Handy hint

Carry an amber amulet (charm). According to Arab doctors – some of the best in the 14th century – it will prevent rheumatism.

Where'd he go?

Aaaaargh!

Dare you argue with an abbot?

Are you courteous, tactful, smooth-talking, clear-headed, calm – and strong-minded? You'll need all these qualities when the time comes to talk to the people who pay for cathedral buildings. They range from kings, queens and local landowners to senior priests and abbots (heads of monasteries). Most will have travelled to Europe and seen fascinating buildings in foreign lands. They may want you to copy them.

All these rich, powerful people are used to getting their own way. They don't like to be contradicted! But you must persuade them that your plan is the best.

Bothersome bishops

CHURCHMEN often have strong views. In 1170, Canterbury's own archbishop, Thomas Becket, was murdered in the cathedral by royal soldiers after a quarrel with King Henry II. Now Becket's buried close to where he died, in a beautiful new chapel.

Local worthies

LEADING LOCAL PEOPLE – lords and ladies, mayors and merchants (left) – are very proud of 'their' cathedral. They are always willing to give money, but like to be consulted in return. Don't hurt their feelings!

Handy hint

Be trustworthy. William the Englishman (see page 21) got the job because he was 'acute (clever) and honest'.

There he goes again...

It's got to be better than anything the French have got.

23

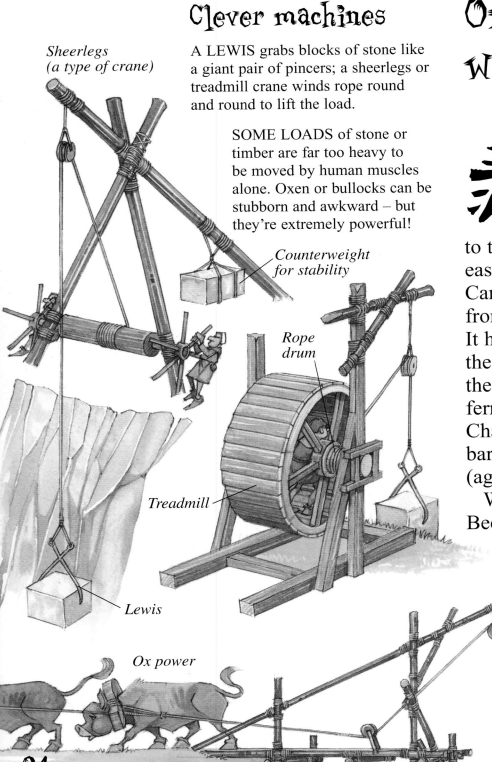

Clever machines

*Sheerlegs
(a type of crane)*

A LEWIS grabs blocks of stone like a giant pair of pincers; a sheerlegs or treadmill crane winds rope round and round to lift the load.

SOME LOADS of stone or timber are far too heavy to be moved by human muscles alone. Oxen or bullocks can be stubborn and awkward – but they're extremely powerful!

*Counterweight
for stability*

*Rope
drum*

Treadmill

Lewis

Ox power

Only the best will do

As master mason, it will also be your job to find building stone for the cathedral, and get it transported to the building site. That's no easy task! The stone for Canterbury comes all the way from Caen in northern France. It has to be hewn into blocks at the quarry, taken by ox-cart to the coast, loaded on ships and ferried across the English Channel, transferred to river barges, then carried on ox-carts (again) for the last mile or two.

Why go to all that trouble? Because Caen stone is some of the best in the world. It's limestone, with a smooth, fine texture and a lovely pale cream colour. And it's what masons call 'freestone', which means it can be cut and carved in any direction without splitting or cracking.

Pestered by pilgrims

L ike all 14th-century Christians, you honour saints and believe that their prayers will help you get to heaven. Canterbury Cathedral houses the relics (remains) of famous local saint Thomas Becket. A gold, jewelled casket in the Trinity Chapel holds his body; the Corona (a circular chapel) contains part of his skull.

Every year, thousands of pilgrims flock to Canterbury to see the relics. Their gifts of money help pay for building work – but these visitors cause problems! They need food, drink, lodgings and entertainment. And all too often, they get rowdy.

Who d'you think you are – the Archbishop of Canterbury?

It should be a best-seller!

Canterbury Tales

MANY PILGRIMS treat their journey as a jolly holiday. They ride fine horses, stay in cosy inns and amuse each other with funny stories. Right now, England's top poet, Geoffrey Chaucer, is composing a collection of such stories.

In 1370, Archbishop Sudbury had to run for his life when angry pilgrims attacked him, after he had scolded them for bad behaviour.

Handy hint

Fire has destroyed many churches and cathedrals – including Canterbury. So be careful where pilgrims leave the candles that are symbols of their prayers.

I shall not be moved.

I wonder how fast he can run in those robes.

Royal resting place

KINGS AND PRINCES pay good money to be buried in the cathedral. Best known is Edward the 'Black Prince', son of King Edward III and husband of local heiress Joan, the 'Fair Maid of Kent'. When this famous warrior died in 1376, Henry Yevele (see page 17) designed a magnificent gold and bronze tomb for him.

He never wore shoes like that, you know. Not while I knew him.

Why was Edward called the Black Prince? Some say that it's because he wore black armour or carried a black shield, but nobody knows for sure.

Building for the future

Well! You've seen what the future might hold if you choose to be a cathedral builder: long years of study, tough tests of skill, hard work, and heavy responsibilities. Are you still really sure that it's the right career for you? If so, good luck! But, before you start, there's one other problem to consider. Could you really devote your life to work that you'll never see completed? Not sure? Then think about this: if you could travel hundreds of years into the future, you'd find that most of Europe's great cathedrals are still standing, proud and beautiful – and are still loved, admired and used for prayers by millions of people.

After you're gone...

I'd make it taller.

WARTIME TARGET. In the 17th century, the English Parliament's army will smash stained glass at Canterbury.* In the 20th, Canterbury's towers will be bombed.

A NEW MASTER MASON will take over. Will he honour your plans and your vision – or have his own new ideas?

LONG YEARS of wind, rain, frost and snow will shatter the strongest stone. By the 21st century, Canterbury Cathedral will need urgent work to save it from falling down!

28

* They were very strict Christians and believed it was sinful to admire beautiful images.

THE CATHEDRAL TODAY contains work of every period from the 11th century to the 19th.

Handy hint

Sign your work. Some masons and carvers even hide pictures of themselves among the carvings.

...and their amazing work is still standing today!

Glossary

Apprentice A young person who learns a trade by working for a master, usually without pay.

Arch An opening in a wall, with a curved top. It is much stronger than a flat-topped opening.

Archbishop A top-ranking bishop with authority over other bishops.

Bishop A senior churchman with authority over ordinary priests.

Budget The amount of money available to spend on a project.

Buttress A strong, heavy prop built against the side of a wall to prevent it from leaning.

Capital A block at the top of a pillar, carved in a decorative shape.

Cathedral A church that is the headquarters of a bishop.

Chapel A smaller place of worship within a church or other building.

Cloister A courtyard with a covered walkway around the edge.

Column A cylindrical pillar.

Flying buttress A buttress that is built some distance away from a wall, and connected to it by half-arches.

Foundation The lowest part of a building, below ground level, which supports the weight of the whole building.

Frieze A band of carved decoration along the surface of a wall.

Guild A society or brotherhood for members of a particular trade or profession. It provides help for members, and may try to prevent non-members from following the trade.

Journeyman A worker who has finished his apprenticeship but has not yet qualified as a master. He is paid by the day, and the name comes from the French word *journée*, meaning 'a day' or 'a day's work'.

Mason A worker who builds in stone.

Master A worker who has passed an examination to prove that he is skilled in his trade. He is allowed to employ other workers and to train apprentices.

Master mason A mason who has qualified as a master; also, the head mason on a building project.

Masterpiece A test-piece made by a worker as part of the examination to become a master.

Molten Melted by heating to a very high temperature.

Monastery The home of a community of monks.

Niche A shallow opening in a wall, usually to hold a statue.

Pilgrim A person who travels to visit holy places and relics.

Pillar A tall, narrow support for a roof or a wall.

Pinnacle A tall, narrow ornament, often on the top of a buttress.

Pulpit The platform on which a priest stands to lead prayers or give a sermon.

Rafter A sloping piece of wood which is part of the structure of a roof.

Relic A part of a saint's body, or an article that belonged to a saint.

Rib A narrow band of stone which helps to strengthen a vault.

Scribe A person who writes or copies official documents.

Shrine A place where a saint is commemorated, especially a place that has relics of the saint.

Template A pattern of wood or metal which is used as a guide for shaping something that needs to be made.

Vault A roof with an arched shape, which is much stronger than a flat or sloping roof.

Index

A
accidents 18–19, 20–21
amulet 21
apprentice 12–13
arch 16–17
archbishops of Canterbury 8, 22, 26–27

B
Becket, St Thomas 8, 22, 26
bell-maker 11
bishop 6
Black Prince 27
buttress 16–17, 19
  flying 18

C
Caen stone 24
Canterbury 5, 6
  Cathedral 8–9, 16–17, 20–21, 26–29
Canterbury Tales 26
cathedra 6
cathedrals of Europe 6–7
chapel 8, 22
Chaucer, Geoffrey 26
cranes 24
crypt 8

D
deviser 10
drawing-floor 18

E
Ely Cathedral 18–19

F
fire 8, 27
freestone 24
frieze 16–17

G
gargoyle 16–17
glazier 11, 20
guilds 11, 13

I
indenture 12

J
journeyman 12, 14–15, 16

L
lewis 24

M
machines 24
mason 10, 12–13, 15, 20
master (skilled mason) 12, 14, 16
master mason (head mason) 18, 20–21, 28
masterpiece 16
maze 16
monasteries, monks 7, 14
money 22–23, 26

N
nave 8

O
oxen 24

P
pilgrims 26–27
pillar 16–17, 19
pinnacle 19
Pisa, Leaning Tower of 19

Q
quarryman 10, 24–25

R
relics 26
rib-vaulting 19
roofer 11, 20

S
stained glass 11, 17, 28
statues 16–17
stone 24–25

T
travel 14–15
treadmill 24

V
vault 8, 19
Villard de Honnecourt 18

W
William the Englishman 21, 23
William of Sens 20–21
woodcarver 10
woodworkers 10

Y
Yevele, Henry 17, 27